Reclaiming the Apple:
Poems from Afghanistan

Adrienne Amundsen

Dedicated to the women, men,
and children of Afghanistan;
to Afghans4Tomorrow;
to our Global Exchange Group Spring 2010;
to Najib Sedeque, our gentle, fearless guide;

and, as always, to my boys.

"Let the world change you, and you can
change the world."
                    —Ernesto "Che" Guevarra

Reclaiming the Apple: Poems from Afghanistan

Adrienne Amundsen

Pech Merle Press

Cover Design by Jim Shubin (ShubinDesign.com)
Cover image by Adrienne Amundsen
Book production by Proforma Mactec Solutions
Author photo, Douglas Coffee
Library of Congress Cataloging-in-Publication Data
Author Name: Adrienne Amundsen
Title: Reclaiming the Apple: Poems from Afghanistan

Printing: Lowry McFerrin
Proforma Mactec Solutions (lowry.mcferrin@proforma.com)

ISBN: 978-0-9852672-2-3

PUBLICATION CREDITS

Another version of "Reciprocal World" was printed in
the journal *RiverOaks Review*.

"And Yet, Chickens," will be in an upcoming edition
of *Spillway*.

"Apple" was published in a revised version as "How
the Apple Tasted to Her" in the online journal
"occupyyourpositivefuture," and is forthcoming in its
original version as "Apple" in the *Schuylkill Valley
Journal*.

"Buzkashi" to appear in *Qwerty Journal*, 2014.

FOREWORD

This slender book of poetry is more than a narrative about a compelling journey to Afghanistan, though it began as such. The geography of outer world and inner reflections that resulted could have become a book, yet it more than suffices as good poetry can do in bringing us the sensory impressions and moral ambiguity that is at the crossroads site of ongoing, perennial war. This volume is the next step toward answering her own question:

"Why would a responsible woman
leave everything to go to a warzone?"

Adrienne Amundsen created an image of a girl out of clay and then in a metaphoric way (as Aphrodite did for Pygmalion's creation) the image came alive and was an Afghan orphan or princess.

She says:
"Come and see,
Come and see."

Amundsen learned that Global Exchange, an international human rights organization was organizing a women's peace mission to Kabul. She felt drawn to go, resisted and regretted. So that when a second opportunity came up, this time she went,

"pulling doubts around me like a woolen cloak."

I work with and write about the idea of responding to "assignments" that are personally meaningful, would be fun—fun has do with using who we are—our talents and experience, and being with people who share our values; and are motivated by love. It's a choice, which can be compelling. I also describe life-threatening illness as a soul journey in which a diagnosis can bring us "close to the bone" or to what we know at a soul level about what matters, who and what we trust, and must do. Whether we heed what we know, is, however, also a choice. I was especially appreciative of Amundsen's description:

"The call came like the sound of a *shofar*,
a vibration in the bones."

Amundsen gave me a sense of what it must be like to be in the shattered city of Kabul or outside the city in the Hindu Kush where "space appears like a miracle," and hills are seen against blue skies. She mentioned that compacted garbage is used for meager heat and the smell of it is in the air of Kabul. On this Global Exchange tour, she saw a tiny baby struggling for life, went shopping at a lapis store, interacted with street kids begging in the street, celebrated International Women's Day with Afghan women, and learned of the existence and what it is like to be in a walled Women's Park, an oasis of green grass and freedom from burkas for privileged women and their children. Some poems look back a year later and bring to mind women she sees in her psychotherapy practice, whose warzone was home, an American father responsible for the ruination of childhood. She muses about death by friendly fire, Pat Tillman's fate in Afghanhistan, troops trained to kill, and children who lead soldiers into IED traps.
"Apple" begins "Afghanistan came through my hands, and I came to her," a reference to the girl she made of clay who called her there. Now after her re-

turn, it is a village girl she saw holding an apple tightly (from "Blue Lapis Tara") who inspires parts of this work of words. *Reclaiming the Apple* is the title of this collection of poems. In "Monster in the Mirror" the girl with the apple asked with her eyes, "What are you here for?"

I loved this collection of poems which tap into my own thoughts and has me muse about Aphrodite's symbol, the apple (may the village girl hold on to and taste love and beauty someday in place of bombs and ruins). Apple also comes to mind (though the Bible never mentions this) as the fruit of the Tree of Knowledge of Good and Evil in the Garden of Eden. It would be good to see through our delusions and know good from evil.

— Jean Shinoda Bolen, M.D.

Author *Goddesses in Everywoman, Urgent Message From Mother*

CONTENTS

THROUGH MY HANDS:
FROM ART TO AFGHANISTAN

Her dark face emerges
from soft brown clay, my fingers
smoothing its slick surfaces.
Her eyes are wide with fear,
her mouth open in a scream.
She wears Afghan fabric,
carries a rolled prayer rug—
all reds and sand—
and her hair is wild black
and scorched.
I call her Afghan princess,
Afghan orphan.
Why do I start telling her story
of loss and wandering and
bombed villages?
I study her country;
I read the histories of failed conquests.
The poets, the stories of kites.
She beckons and tells me to come.

And then our towers fall.
We bomb Afghanistan.
She is collateral damage,
but look at her:

She is herself, the princess,
the orphan, her face in
a rictus of fear,

and I see in her scream
a doorway to war's mad
history, its nexus there

in the desert crossroads.
Maybe this is the place
where powerbrokers
meet the devil and make that deal—
not the road in the American south
where the bluesman roamed.
Music may be devilish,
but the oil men
and Armageddon makers
are the real devil.

She says,
"Come and see,
come and see."

THE CALL: IF I HAD GONE

I strain against the yoke.
I am old and cranky and
need to be free.
There are journeys to take.
Hecate enters my psyche,
crisps my soft edges,
narrows my eyes.
I cackle
when formerly
I crooned.

Why else would a
responsible woman
leave everything,
go to a war zone?
I don't know who I am anymore,
hatching from the husk
of Mother to a new form,
metamorphosis incomplete.
New stories in my head,
new calls to action
in a world wild again with war.

She comes into my dreams—
the Afghan orphan I made from clay.
She calls me time and again,
and I would be on my way back tonight,
had I gone to Afghanistan.

There was a peace delegation,
but I turned back.

I would be on my way back tonight,
but my heart shaped itself in
familiar contours around those I love,
crooned again her lullabies.
I made love to safety.

Then that rumbling erupted again,
and it has groaned for days
at my cowardice, my restraint.

Other women are coming home now,
warriors for love,
returning with their stories.
And I am here, still here,
poised to go.

The Call:
On Finally Going to Afghanistan

This time I stride resolutely out the door,
suitcase packed for days.
No more asking for advice.
Though a bomb ripped through a Kabul guesthouse,
I'm not backing out again.

A little like a soldier, just a little,
decision made and danger beckoning ...
no more wavering,
just pulling my doubts around me
like a woolen cloak,
tidying its folds and wrinkles,
stilling my eyes, my breathing.
I walk through security, show my ticket
marked "Kabul," leaving no opening for
suspicious looks or questions.

The call came like the sound of a *shofar*,
a vibration in the bones.
I am supposed to do this.
A magnetic force pulled
the iron in my blood to
the eye of the storm.
This is what everything has come to.
The chickens are not home to roost
but are wandering the streets, hungry.

It is the place where the crossroads
became the crosshairs,
the armed chessboard,

postmodern war games,
what humans have made.
From this place I will look,
and I will see what has come to pass,
and where I stand in the great unraveling,
or the great unfolding.

And I will try to tell you what I learned ...
and didn't learn.

When the call comes
it is not a shiny rainbow
enticing you; it is not
the dulcet tones of
fairy pipes, nor
the trumpet of
uniformed certainty.
It is a roiling belly,
nausea and vertigo,
it is night sweats and
friends' warnings,
it is an electric current
too strong for your body
and a fierce light
shining from your forehead,
and you try to turn it off,
turn your attention
back to reading the newspaper,
vacuuming the cat hair from
the old carpet,
paying the bills.
You press your nose
to your familiar grindstone

but this call keeps sounding,
sounding, till you lift up
your head and say,
"May I refuse?" and it
says, "You may, but then
your blood will thin,
your will sour, your
heart weigh heavier
in your chest."
And you say, "I see,
yes, I see,"

and you say, "yes."

KABUL SUITE, 2010

I.

All I see is brown, broken.
Houses everywhere are broken walls.
This is what bombs do.
Every bomb a home,
a family, a body,
flesh and bone and blood,
bloody clothes on an unpaved street—
packed life stories spilling out of their bags
onto streets now garbage dumps.

The Kabul River
is clogged with rebar and plastic bags,
far from its pure mountain source.
Children cower,
taking shelter from the rain,
finding floor above the mud,
while bombs explode
and rockets aim for the Parliament member
riding down Jalalabad Road.

Where is the poem in a war zone?
Do I dishonor the dead or
the pain of the living
with my search?
This is the place where poems die,
this graveyard of nations,
this charnel ground.

I am in another universe.
Hungry for meaning,
I find only the crash of soul upon stone

and the strange smell of garbage
burned for meager heat.
War's detritus is condensed.
Dense layers of the concrete
crush the nuance of the poetic.

Where is the grass?
Where there is so much to fix,
why do I come back to grass?
I long to see barren parks filled with green,
street children running on something soft,
see mothers sit and lovers stroll,
battered people resting
their eyes on something
that is not broken.

Where are the birds?
The trees are filled with rustling brown pods,
but they are empty.
Brown trees in brown parks
are empty of birds.
Fruit stands and tailor shops
line the muddy streets.
Sometimes a cage is hung for canaries.
You can't hear their songs
above the roar of busses and trucks,
and I wonder how they breathe
in this fume-filled air,
song and color in the dust.

II.

One morning we rise early,
ride the bus outside the city's confines,
out where space appears like
a miracle, hills open to the blue skies,

and the road rises toward the Hindu Kush.
We rise up into air
as fresh as the earth's beginning,
and the songs of birds fall
upon our startled ears.
They lift in flocks
above the mercifully unruined hills.
On the brown hillside
a blue-domed mosque looms
above the mud-brick houses,
and graveyards bloom
with blue-crossed graves.

There is still a sound
besides that of war and machines,
but it is fleeing,
running from us
with our bankrupt notions
of good and evil.

III.

In the rough hospital
there is a tiny baby
sprawled on his back,
half-wrapped in a worn white blanket,
eyes closed and mouth open,
his little chest rising and falling
like that of a fallen bird.
I can't take my eyes away.
I had a boy like that;
he did not live.
In this ruin of a city,
what chance does this one have?
Will his mother carry him home alive,
or return with empty arms?

Does she have a home or just the street,
or one of the houses
thrown up on the gray hillside
above the city,
where carrying water home
could be a full day's job?

We end up at a lapis store—
boisterous Americans
in the ancient bazaar.
We buy bowls, hats, earrings,
sweep aside our somber moods
with beauty and good deals.
Outside on Chicken Street,
the unpaved road is piled with garbage,
and street kids pound on the door—
"Hey, you; I be your bodyguard!
I show you something more special!"
All day our guide has kept us safe.
Cell phone to his ear, he
fixes meetings, tracks danger
and streets to avoid.
"You will be safe," he tells us.
"And we will pray, *Inshallah*,
for the bombs to stop."

Inside, now, as we hum about the store,
he bows in the corner to pray,
a delicate man of impeccable dignity,
prostrate on his blood-red rug.
All around him is light.

IV.

At day's end,
street children sell gum to survive,

and a toothless woman crouches
by the road, surrounded by crowds,
a hard loaf of bread set before her
like an offering.
Bread for sale,
indistinguishable from the mud
in which she sits.

There is a thick mist in the early evening.
Dusk is falling and our bus passes fruit stalls
lining the muddy river;
they are lit by strings of fluorescent lights
in misty rainbow colors,
soft in the wet nightfall,
curled spiral lights of blue and pink and spring green,
these lights everywhere
defying the carnage.
I could linger for hours,
looking past the debris
at such sweet seductive glow.
But I must be locked behind doors after dark,
guarded by men with guns.

Here is what we do at night:
eat spicy rice and kabobs,
drink Coke,
shower in whatever water we have that day,
thrilled if it's hot.
We load the metal stoves
with composted briquettes.
The smell they give off is incomparable,
somewhere between incense and garbage.
I have grown fond of the smell
and know I cannot take it home.
We imagine what is happening in the streets,
where we are not allowed to go—

life and death and everything in between.
"Do not go on the roof," they tell us;
"bad neighbors."
So we gather in the safety we make
in this new family we forge
in the middle of war.

V.

A bomb rocked our guest house last night.
I slept through it.
I fear for my family at home,
grow inured to danger to myself.
Have I abandoned my boys, my husband?
Why am I here?
I can learn but I cannot fix.
I do not want my children to be orphans
like the boys at the bus window
waving buckets of holy smoke for sale—
"One dollah!" they call.
They gesture dismissively when we decline.
Some of the buckets don't even have smoke,
but the boys wave them exuberantly,
then aggressively—
"Buy! Buy!"—
and bang the windows if we do not.

Holy smoke,
bless us all this smoggy
sunny day where cars and busses wheel
in traffic circles and we
suddenly break free
and careen forward to follow
the military caravan.

VI.

Princes strut on their
prancing horses, jostle each other
and the lesser men,
all leather and fur,
red coats and dark faces.
Buzkashi! In ancient China,
captured men were the ball.
Now they use a goat carcass.
Everything is brutal—
rough hand on the reins
jerks at the bit in the horse's mouth,
lathered, bleeding at the corners.
The men run for raw meat lying
in the dirt, covered with flies,
lean over like ancient polo players,
grab it and race in wild circles.
Small boys patrol the stands,
scope out us foreigners.
"Hey, soldier,
cigarettes?"
So slowly we are moving
toward love,
or maybe not even that.
The horses do as they are asked,
carrying men to battle,
even in games.

VII.

The women at the celebration
hand us emerald-green scarves
inscribed in Dari.
Women in suits and women in burqas
take our hands, eyes shining, say,

"Congratulations
on International Women's Day!"
We are searched by men, by dogs,
and finally by other women,
in a small room with a blanket for a door.
A veiled woman gently pats me down,
puts her arms around me to check all sides.
She smiles, I smile back—
rare touch in this modest and fearful place.
I want to hug her,
say,"Sister! Mother!"
but we both pull back when the search is over.
I wear my green scarf
like a medal they have won,
and given to me.

Then there is a walled women's park
rimmed by men with guns
who search us before we enter.
Women in soft blue burqas
stroll in, covered,
then shed their veils,
throw them back and burst into glorious bloom
of satin, lamé, brash colors
and gold jewelry,
full lips burnished red and copper,
dark hair gleaming beneath the shadowed sun.

In purple high heels they
walk in their park,
children in arms or
toddling by their sides.
There is grass here, small
patches of it, scraggly and browned,
in some places even green.

I imagine its tough stringy roots
pushing through clay, reaching
for water, a fragile net forming
underground.

Here under the dusty Kabul sky
children are laughing on swings.
Women on benches
whisper secrets
in each others' jeweled ears.

VIII.

The kites are back on the hill in Kabul's core
after years of banishment.
It is Sunday and the men are out
with their sons,
buying rainbow kites,
strings coated with glass,
one kite fighting another.
Bright colors against a bright blue sky,
happy kids and happy families.
Playful war in the clear blue sky,
on the hill above the ruins.
Tomorrow more bombs will fall.
Women will sell bread on the streets,
brave girls go to school.
Elders will grieve,
and warriors will tear the goat
limb
from
limb.

OM

The stars above the high desert at night
shine down in breathless beauty,
but I cannot see them.
I am locked inside,
guarded by armed men.
The Refugees sleep
in houses with walls,
taking their chances.

In the morning the sun pushes itself
through rainclouds, drying
the Kabul mud.
I hover above myself
and watch us, driven around
this shattered city in a white bus
with a rainbow-colored *om*
painted on the front.

Om: creation, preservation,
destruction. The sound of the world,
making and unmaking.
Everywhere I look I am learning.

Fundamentalists inner and outer.
There is a Taliban in my psyche,
white-turbaned and kohl-eyed,
ready to pounce, to shut me down,
to torture me for the crime of
being visible. It is shameful
even to think such arid thoughts,
to cruise the wasteland of
my inner world when real
Land Rovers raced around this city
and chopped off women's fingers for
the crime of being painted.

Still, inner and outer stare at each other,
a fierce and puzzled mirror.
I left a wasteland at home, too.
My work is like a MASH unit,
women tortured by
their upright American fathers,
still trembling decades after
being raped. Someone I love
is drowning in sickness, driven by
demons I have tried to but cannot erase.

The brokenness here is so big
I am brought to my knees.
It is so big that I am free to
sit in the white bus and
give up trying to even imagine solutions.
 I am free to marvel
at the soft lights in the late
afternoon rain; I surrender to
the sounds of foreign voices,
their rise and fall a new wall
upon which I lean, taking in
the smells of composted briquettes
burning in metal stoves and loosing
their smoke into the late winter air.
My heart is tight with sorrow and prayer.

I always thought I could do more.
but that thought falls away.
Bombs down the road,
the *om* on the front of the bus,
too big to fix,
too big to fix.
I am alone; I am free;
now, there is nothing I can do.

LOOK WHAT HAPPENS

Pat Tillman sits against
the boulder he chose to save him,
head deflated like an
emptied bowl,
blood and brain pouring from
holes like a river
through a breaking dam.
Bullets ricocheted inside his skull,
turned fine mind into liquid
pouring now into Afghan soil,
soaking his friend's hands, his arms,
while the friend screams.

Down the hill, his own men shoot—
mad, misled, unmanaged.
Radios spit careless commands.
Words split from sense—
"Go! Go! Go!
Split the platoon! Fire!"
Two halves of one troop
have lined up as ordered,
facing each other,
as though for a classical dance,
there on the far fringe of meaning,
guns raised and blazing.
They shoot their brothers,
again, and again, and again.

Pat Tillman sits against
the boulder he thought would save him.
Fourteen minutes of noise,
then silence.
Darkness draws near.
Soldiers pant,
racing minds slow,

the sound of gunfire echoes
in their boyish ears.
Hearts pound, settle.
Hawks reel overhead, keening.
Flies begin to buzz
around this new carrion,
land on his once-beautiful face.

Look what happens there in the wadi
strewn with rocks and boulders,
this narrow pass.
Here at the far edges of empire,
tattered people, tattered clothes,
tattered convoys,
all pull at the loose threads
of some vast fabric
thinking to reweave but
only unraveling, unraveling,
back to desert and tribe and blood.

We shouldn't be here,
near a village where kids run
barefoot down dusty streets.
Each child
another small human packet,
seedbed full of flowers
ready to bloom,
likely to die.
Here women bake,
and men buy weapons
to keep out this year's invaders.
They are too close to tanks, M-3's,
SAWS, missile launchers—
the strange words of war—
and so, it turns out,
are the Americans
carrying them.

Look what happens here in the wadi—
too many weapons,
words flying like bullets,
bullets flying to kill.

What do we do with our heroes?
A man of muscle,
with a mind for justice,
sees his people jump from
tall towers slammed by
planes like missiles.
He says, "Somebody's gotta do something
and I'm a man to do it."
Star of the gridiron,
he leaves the game.
He's a brave man, willing to sacrifice.
But what use are heroes
when the stories are corrupt
and their country is a war machine?
Voices pour through the airwaves
chanting, "Hero, hero, hero,"
but they mean something else.

Pat Tillman says,"They're lying.
What are we doing here?"

He sits by the boulder
he thought would save him.
Our soldier boys
did as they were told
and shot each other.
What are we doing here?
Look what happens here in the wadi.
Flies are buzzing,
words flying like bullets,
bullets flying to kill.

TRAINED TO KILL

This is what happens.
He wakes from his fractured sleep,
head emptying.
Trained to kill: It fills him.
What did you expect?
Alcohol to soothe the pain,
now, shutting down the censors,
nothing left but *trained to kill*,
brain damaged by bomb concussions.
He saw his buddy killed last week.
The dust is getting to him,
and the hate the locals feel.
He's got kids at home and a wife
waiting like Penelope for her warrior
to return. He returns,
but they keep sending him back.
Endless war, just like Ender's,
just like Orwell's;
it used to seem like science fiction;
now it's real—just far away.
Take those young people
with not much future,
send them off to kill
the folks who live on top of oil,
along with terrorists
crazed by poverty and war.
So he was sent off four times,
and this time the fractures went too deep, and
he did what he was trained to do.

Seventeen Afghans—
women, children, men—
lying there now with flies

sticking to the blood
on their robes,
parents screaming.
This is what happens.

Cluster fuck, endgame,
mutually assured destruction—
spirit leaves in war.
Bales is court-martialed.
Afghan children lie lifeless in the sun.

Trained to kill.

AND YET, CHICKENS

Everybody loves chickens,
their clucks and feathers
and eggs,
and even, yes,
their sweet bodies
whose meat keeps
a hungry Afghan family alive.
A simple thing, to fill
a woman's home
with chickens—
now she walks proud
through the streets of her town,
purveyor of chickens.
Her husband bows to her—
well, at least he does not beat her—
for his wife is the woman
with poultry, the woman with money,
the woman he needs.

Schools for Girls

And all the while,
girls in their clean white scarves
sit in bare classrooms, copying letters,
serious faces turned down, pencils scurrying
across precious paper, reading stories
and memorizing poems. They proudly
recite for visitors in English.
"I will be a doctor!" "A pilot!"
"A teacher!" "A mother!"
"The President!" Their hands
are red and chapped with cold,
but after class they embroider purses
with sequins to earn money for their school.
The schools have to move after bomb threats.
Teachers move the letter charts
to another room in somebody's house.
They stay ahead of the bombs,
if they're lucky.
They slip like small fish
in a trilling stream, hide
beneath rocks and in the
grasses, waiting
till the danger passes.

THREE COATS #2

I.

Young men guide him by the elbow
to his scratched leather chair
in the cool room where we wait.
Parliamentarian now,
or so they say, but
Taliban chief before,
he wears a stained
white turban, his face is
chiseled as from stone, harsh,
and his left eye is blind, milky,
unfocussed beneath heavy
black glasses, like
Elvis Costello's but taped
at the earpiece, resting
awkwardly askew on his nose.
His dark beard flows
down onto a magnificent coat,
satin emerald-green, striped with
the purple of kings.
It falls to his feet and
fills the drab room with color.

"What do you have to say
about the women?" my fierce
friend spits, eyes narrow
and blazing. "What do you have to say?"
His voice is deep and measured.
"Mistakes were made," his
translator says. "Mistakes
were made." The ex-Marine
leans toward him in near-lust,
two former warriors facing off,
barely restraining themselves,

discussing peace.
We file out and he offers himself,
stands posing with each of us,
straight and unmoving,
and when I am next to him
he points to my coat,
long black wool with
golden designs.
"Tajik?" he asks.
"No, California," I say.
The translator says:
"He likes your coat."
And I reply: "Tell him
I like his coat too."
The camera catches us
standing stiffly side by side,
he in his coat,
I in mine.

A year later I hear he is dead.
The shooter could be anybody—
Taliban killing their turncoat,
someone whose son he killed,
American soldier. By accident or design,
who knows?
There are endless reasons
for vengeance.

II.

I am thinking about that coat.
We have travelled into the foothills
of the snowy Kush,
to the town of Istalaf,
where narrow stalls line
a dusty road, stores full of clothes,

vases, lapis, and bowls.
In the back of a dark market
stall I see that coat hanging,
shadowed green
and the purple of ripe grapes.
I robe myself and preen,
push up the long sleeves,
turn, laughing, and my new
friends say, "You have to buy it!"
It hangs in my closet now,
too wild for my life,
eggplant and emerald,
chartreuse, satin, violet,
the purple of desire—
the coat of the chieftan,
spoils of war.

III.

Such a little prince, he
struts with his hands on his hips,
barely taller than his mother's knees.
She is walking on,
tossing off her burqa as
she enters the women's park,
but he stands, expecting his due:
admiration. In his royal coat of
purple and green, he flashes
mischievous black eyes
and dares us to doubt his
power, his fire.
                    Who will he
become? Warrior, kohl-eyed
Taliban suicide bomber,
educated guide for American visitors,
mujahidin, council member,

loving father? A good man
or evil? Mostly we are all
a jumble but sometimes,
in a place shredded by wars,
it is more stark. Power
turns perverse; courage
and rage turn to terrorism;
young men, whose
bodies surge with rising
manhood, explode
like the bombs that killed
their neighbors, their
families.
        What choices
will he make, this princely
boy, robed in his long, striped
coat? Green like the grasses
absent from this barren place,
purple-blue like the lapis
lining the cracks beneath the earth,
vivid against the dust and debris,
it pulses life, life, life.

KITE HILL, KABUL, 2010

The man on the hill
where the kites fly
stops his cart filled with
mountains of cashews and almonds.
Scented steam rises from the nuts
as though they were small volcanoes,
dormant but hot.
And the moment he stops,
hordes of children dragging their kites
circle round,
chattering to me in Dari.
"Please buy for me; buy for me!"

I buy a small cone of cashews
and am the instant center
of a small galaxy of boys,
jostling, wheedling, finally getting cross.
I am down to my last afghani,
broke—like a Westerner,
not like an Afghan.
And I am learning the hard way
the dangers of the infinite yes;
before you know it you are drowning,
and they are still hungry.
I smile sadly and shake my head,
walk down the hillside
where the kites are flying
and fathers spread picnic blankets
with their children—boys, a few girls.

The hill has been liberated—
no more Taliban laws against play—
but still, mostly, the women don't come.
Liberation has its limits.
I face the sky and eat.

Hunger and sorrow,
longing and rage,
weariness and hope,
families of men and boys, kites—
red and blue and yellow and green—
the wild blue sky,
the barren city below,
broken to pieces by war,
war, and more war.
It is a ceasefire here on kite hill,
and kids run laughing while their kites
lift into the wind.

Bless it all,
bless it all,
and the man with his cart with
its hill of salted nuts.
See it now as it could be:
every stomach full,
girls and mothers everywhere,
tanks gone and the guns all
mysteriously jammed,
as though our common will spoke
to the vibratory universe.

Listen to the sound of a land without fear.
Listen to the sound of a land without armies.
Listen to the sound of women laughing
with the men.
I hear the sound of the wind catching the kites,
the crackle and the boom
when the wind lifts the paper.
I hear boys talking in voices like songs,
and below, the sound of traffic,
almost like a river.

Every moment is a poem,
every poem a prayer.

APPLE

Knowing as I know that war is killing children
while I sit here on the deck at Nepenthe,
do I dare to enjoy the crows on the railing,
the boundless blue sea
whose beauty invented words?

How do I join the Christmas shoppers,
indulge in memories
of the youthful, sex-drenched
life when I first came here to Big Sur,
wishing that girl still alive in this life-worn body?
In Kabul now the winter is coming.
and most people don't have heat.
Any minute a bomb could be dropped,
a rocket launched,
somebody's life smashed to blood and dust,
while I sit on the sunwashed deck
where last I wrote, haunted, about my brother's death.

It will never stop.

The crow sits still now,
right in my view,
pointing his beak so it reflects the sun.
There were almost no birds in Kabul,
but the mountains rose, snow-capped,
into a thin blue sky,
cradling the rubble-strewn city.
In the mountains lived a girl
with dark suspicious eyes,
holding a red apple,
holding it tight,
staring me down.
Every day I wonder
how the apple tasted to her,
if she is still alive.

MONSTER IN THE MIRROR

A year has gone
and it still lives
all through me:
miasma, beautiful
wasteland, the girl's
face, her fierce, sad
eyes, her question:
"What are you here for?"
I still can't tell her,
only that someone should see,
should live with the
ruination. We need an
antidote for hubris,
the monster in the mirror.
What if there was no witness?
This is what we have done.

Deconstructing *we* is
a full-time job.

DELUSION

She sits in my office
weeping silently
telling of her young
husband, a month married.
He said, "They love us,
we are the good guys!"
He said, "We give them
candy, and fix their schools."

"I didn't understand
the Army life,"
she says, face soaked
with sorrow,
"I thought 'you are crazy,
you are not their friend',
but I didn't say that."
And one of the children
took him by the hand
and led him to the house,
to the IED that blew off his legs,
twisted his hands,
shocked his brain,
and now he crawls
on stumps and torso
to the shower
while she pulls her face
into a mask to keep
them both strong. And he says,
"Don't leave me,"
and she says to him, "I

didn't understand
the Army life
and if I stay I will die.
I am young
and you are young."
And this is what it comes to,
this foolish war—
men and children with weapons.
It could be the girl
with the apple; it
could be the luminous
schoolgirls in uniform,
in white scarves,
or street kids selling gum.
We are not their friends
when we come with weapons,
no matter what we tell ourselves.

BLUE LAPIS TARA

I heard they were seeking me in the deserts,
among the stones, the cold rivers.
I heard they couldn't find me
for all the fierce gods roaming the roads,
who blow through the desert
like storm-driven winds,
all cruel eyes and ravenous teeth.
Dionysus denied becomes vicious,
and the father gods, oh,
they are gorged on power.

But still some furrow their brows,
stare through the stinging sand,
faces half-shielded by scarves
of red and teal and green.
Women have survived centuries of this.
They harbor hope beneath their burqas,
plans behind their veils,
and they are seeking me
though they are thrown into prison
for the crime of being raped,
though they feed their children scraps
from the streets strewn with garbage.
They kindle fierce fire in
deathless hearts
and shine its light out
into the barren land
where I do still live,
hidden. You must know
where to look.

Do you see the women gathered
in the great hall, a sea of bright headscarves,
a music of voices,

proud to be women in this city
guarded by guns and dogs?
Do you see the women wearing
their green scarves of independence
and shaking our hands
with pride and solidarity?
Did you hear the young girl,
already a council member in her village,
tell us she will one day be President?

I see the red-clad girls
doing their round kicks, sparring,
Tae Kwon Do team spinning and jumping
and shouting *hae-yah!*
I am in the Olympic court
where the girls practice hoops,
aim for the Games, their
fierce young captain orchestrating
her team as they show their moves
to clumsy old Americans who fall
back, abashed by the purity of their joy.

And oh, look in the dark eyes of the village girl.
She holds her apple tightly, holds your gaze,
mistrustful but standing her ground.
She dares you to make her a symbol
when she is so wholely herself.
Does her life hold hope or disaster?
I sing through the blood in her veins,
I speak in the fierceness of her eyes,
I am the apple she clutches and
the power in her hands.
The mullah holds court down the hill
in the terrace around the mosque,
advises the men,
but she holds her place, and there are days

when I do nothing but spin around her,
spinning round and round her
to protect her from the havoc in this land,
and I am the fire behind those eyes
holding you in their grip.
I have cried so many tears
as I watched this space between empires—
this place made to be free, cooled by the
snows of the Kush with which I ringed you,
watered by my rivers, where I gave you
peaches and carrots, grains and greens,
all you would need. I gave you carpet-makers,
and the imagination to give the carpets flight.
I gave you poets and ecstatic dancers.
Now their temples stand broken on the mountain tops,
where winds blow cold through empty arches.

I watched my land become a warfield,
a charnel ground, a great pawn;
I watched men in white with heads inflated
call upon their God while beating my girls,
my women, using my boys, madness in
their eyes, and I watched as they hacked at
Buddha's statues, all the holy places,
and I wept and I wept and I wept so long
and filled the stony land with so many tears
that they made rivers, deep blue rivers,
flowing and branching everywhere beneath
my body, this land.

The tears have frozen now; they are stone.
They are the lapis you mine for your jewelry,
and if you hold the blue stones close,
if you listen with all your heart,
you will hear me,
the Tara of Blue Lapis.

You will hear me as I whisper still,
"Do not despair,
my children; do not despair.
I am only waiting to be reborn,
and you are carrying my pieces
until they can again come together,
and I will rise up again in the mountains
above you, smiling at last to be whole
in this land of snow, this land where souls
once knew how to dance."

RECIPROCAL WORLD

The freeway exit to my home
opens to a great pasture
where cows graze
and the moon hangs heavy at night,
grass every shade of green in every hour's light,
the pale blue of morning,
sundown's dusty rose,
the black indigo of night.
The pasture is different since I wrote
its poem of silvery moonlight and
bursting udders.
Now a pasture inside me is illuminated
and it has changed me,
the way the rivers of my nerves fire,
the way my eyes open to the light
and my body vibrates
encountering the world.

As I drive through this world,
driving, driving,
the driven life, the daily rounds,
I pass poems everywhere.
There, the freeway sings that told me
to write its story,
how it marks the passing of canyons
and coyotes and wild horses.
The road is mapped now by the stories
it used me to tell,
and everywhere, now,
I can see insignificant asphalt
in the real world of birds,
where human folly is a jagged
background noise.

The egrets told me to speak for them
and because I did
they have welcomed me
into the kinship of their yellow legs,
their whiteshining wings
and sharp steady gaze,
so that when their priests part the curtain
I am allowed into the inner sanctum
where I can see sky all around as we fly,
note the sensation of damp dawn pasture
and the bitter crunch of insects,
the sweet sustaining marrow of their juices.
Because I wrote the egret's poem,
I can see it rising like angel light
over the fields where the white bird
follows the cows.

The poetic world I inhabit fills me
as the unwritten world does not.
Is the world itself changed?
Do poems rise
with the egret from the field,
whose song she asked me to translate?

Purple-flowered vines spoke to me
from my back door one night,
and their poem took me all the way to Africa.
On a windy night they blew in,
the vines and Africa.
They came together riding
into my house, into my body's
suddenly star-studded
matrix of sense and sound and story.
Warriors' horses came racing
with dark tales of turbulence,
and now there is a poem woven

from my open door to Darfur.
From the dry Sudanese ground
darkened with blood,
the poem seeded riotous vines
as it shaped into words
the tears of children taken for soldiers.
Reciprocal alchemy:
A new being shimmers at my back door
and inside me,
since I heard the song of the vineseeds.
The inescapable turbulence of life
lives in violet rivers
in the pulsing network of my veins.

Do I dare to believe that a new being
might rise from the murderous Sudanese plain,
a violet light illumine the places of slaughter?

Afghanistan came through my hands,
and I came to her. If I write of her lapis
and the horror of war, do I knit a skein
of gold to shine upon her sorrow
so that we all circle round her
and sing to her of peace?
If I write of the girl with the apple,
does she live?

Do I create the world
even as it makes me?
I send a desperate prayer out
into the body of the world,
pressing for transformation
whenever the poem wakes up,
stretches, and opens its curtains to the sun.
I call upon the wild wind:
Fill my world with egrets.

Clear the air of keening ghosts.
Make space for life to quicken.
Bring great purple blossoms
to the village broken by war,
and songs to the lips of the children.

Acknowledgements

First, Linda Watanabe McFerrin, who has shep-
herded this collection and believed in it, and in me.
And to Lowry McFerrin, whose technical skills al-
lowed the book to come into form. I am grateful to
Global Exchange, for their progressive vision that
made it possible for me to go to Afghanistan, and to
Afghans 4 Tomorrow, for giving me the chance to see
more closely into the lives of Afghan people living in
their challenged country. I am grateful to my family
and friends, always, and to Ben, Luke, Jackson, and
Doug, for teaching me about love.

About the Author

Adrienne Amundsen is a psychologist, specializing in trauma, grief, and creativity. Born in Texas, but long ago transplanted to northern California, she is the mother of two grown boys. Her poetry has been published in a number of literary journals and anthologies, and her poetry collection *Cassandras Falling* was published in 2011. Dr. Amundsen's interests have taken her from the caves of France to the war zone in Afghanistan, and she has taught classes on shamanism and cave art both locally in California and internationally. She works with a local nonprofit organization, Afghans 4 Tomorrow, which helps Afghans provide girls' education and economic opportunities for families.